Contents

AF711366

目 錄

奇妙中文
Discovering Chinese

The Language

The Chinese spoken language is mainly comprised of Putonghua (Mandarin Chinese or huá yǔ) and local dialects. About one billion Chinese speak Putonghua. Students are taught in Putonghua in schools. Variations of Putonghua, which are called dialects, are used in different parts of China.

The Writing

Chinese writing was first created over three thousand years ago, making it one of the world's oldest living languages. The earliest form of Chinese writing was found on turtle shells, which were used to predict the future.

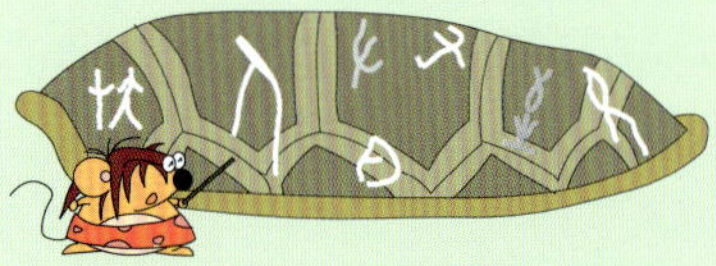

A good part of modern Chinese characters was developed from images of nature, such as the Sun (日), the Moon (月), mountains (山), rivers (川), etc. These symbols, also called "pictograms," evolved over time and gradually became the characters people use today.

Many other characters were derived from a combination of different forms, including the sound they represent. There are over eighty thousand written Chinese characters. On average, a fluent speaker today uses about 1,000 to 2,000 words in everyday living.

The structure of a Chinese word or character can be composed of one part, two or more parts. Examples of characters that consist of one part are: zhōng (中), dà (大), xiǎo (小). Two part characters are written either top-down like jiān (尖), or left-right like lín (林). Three part characters may have the components lined up horizontally like xiè (謝), shù (樹), or vertically like sēn (森).

Chinese words are often made up of two or more simple characters. The dominant character, which sometimes provides a clue as to what the words means, is called the radical. For example, the character lín (林) meaning forest, has the radical mù (木), which means wood. Most words with the radical mù have something to do with wood, like zhuō (桌), which means desk and desks are likely made of wood.

There are eight basic strokes in writing Chinese: héng (横), shù (豎), diǎn (點), piě (撇), nà (捺), tí (提), gōu (鉤) and zhé (折).

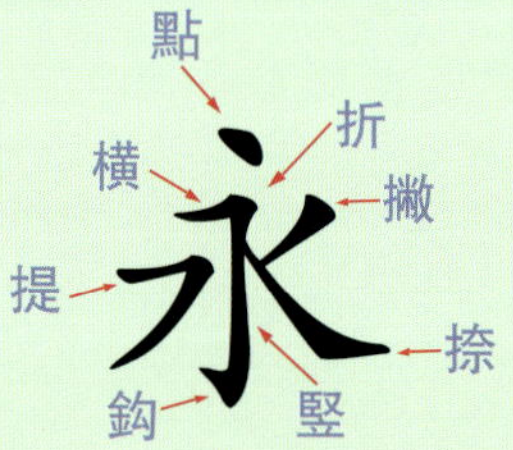

In the old days, Chinese characters were written from top to bottom and from right to left on a page. Today most people and publications have adopted the more international and prevalent writing and printing format that goes horizontally from left to right, just like English.

The Pronunciation

Chinese is spoken with four different tones. The first tone is high and even, like when you open your mouth for the doctor ("Ah...ah"). The second rises in pitch, like when you ask a question ("What?"). The third dips and then rises, like when you are uncertain ("Maybe!?"). The fourth tone is a sharp falling tone. It is short, strong and straight like when you say a forceful "No!"

For more information, visit the "Educators" section at www.BetterChinese.com

tāmen nǎlǐ

第二十五課　它們在哪裡？

第二十五課　它們在哪裡？

課　文 Text

miàn
筆記本在哪裡？筆記本在桌子上面。

書包在哪裡？書包在椅子下面。

bīngxiāng lǐ
蘋果在哪裡？蘋果在冰箱裡面。

xīguā wài
西瓜在哪裡？西瓜在冰箱外面。

lǎoshǔ diànnǎo qián
老鼠在哪裡？老鼠在電腦前面。

hòu
花貓在哪裡？花貓在電腦後面。

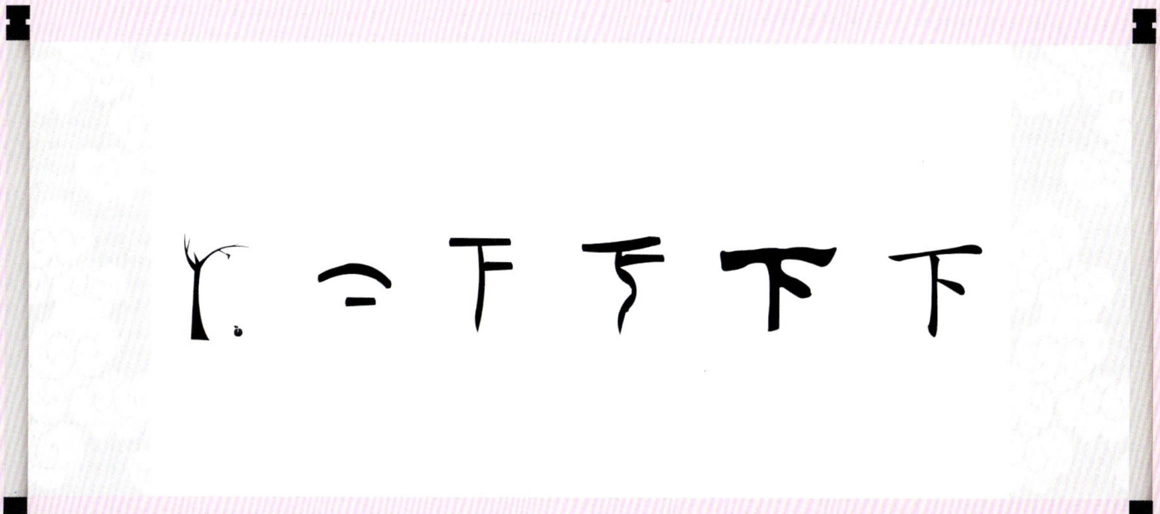

語 法 Grammar

在哪裡？

When asking where something is located, you can say …在哪裡？or …在哪兒？

本子在哪裡？ Where is the notebook?	本子在桌子上面。 The notebook is on the desk.
黑狗在哪裡？ Where is the black dog?	黑狗在椅子下面。 The black dog is under the chair.
他們在哪裡？ Where are they?	他們在汽車裡面。 They are in the car.

句 型 練 習 Exercises

在桌子上面有一個本子。

椅子、下面、書包 ⇨ ______________________________。

冰箱、裡面、香蕉 ⇨ ______________________________。

沙發、後面、籃球 ⇨ ______________________________。

我家、前面、公園 ⇨ ______________________________。

電腦前面是什麼？

學校、後面 ⇨ ______________________________？

本子、上面 ⇨ ______________________________？

冰箱、外面 ⇨ ______________________________？

桌子、下面 ⇨ ______________________________？

書包在椅子下面嗎？

西瓜、冰箱、外面⇨ ______________________________ ？

花狗、汽車、裡面⇨ ______________________________ ？

妹妹、門、外⇨ ______________________________ ？

試試看 Challenge

上面是書，下面是鉛筆，
桌子的上上下下都有文具；
裡面是蘋果，外面是西瓜，
冰箱的裡裡外外都有水果；
前面是花貓，後面是黑狗，
電視機的前前後後都有動物。

◆生字詞

文具 wén jù stationery

浙江・西塘
Xitang Landscape, Zhejiang Province

讀一讀 Reading

春天在哪裡？春天在哪裡？
春天在我們的眼睛裡，
看見紅的花，看見綠的草，
還有會唱歌的布穀鳥。

五福圖 清朝（1616—1911）
Happiness, Qing Dynasty.

◆生字詞

春天	chūn tiān	spring
看見	kàn jiàn	to see
唱歌	chàng gē	to sing a song
布穀	bù gǔ	cuckoo bird
花	huā	flower
草	cǎo	grass
還	hái	also, still

Discovering China

文化

Square Beijing 方方正正的北京

Beijing is shaped rather like a big square slab of tofu. Everything from the wide boulevards to the narrow alleys run straight north and south and east and west. If you do find a road that is slanting, it will always be specially labeled. For example, "Yandai Crooked Street（煙袋斜街）." Streets and alleys divide Beijing into one square block after another. This grid of blocks not only influences the daily lives of Beijing people, but some people believe that it also influences Beijinger's thoughts!

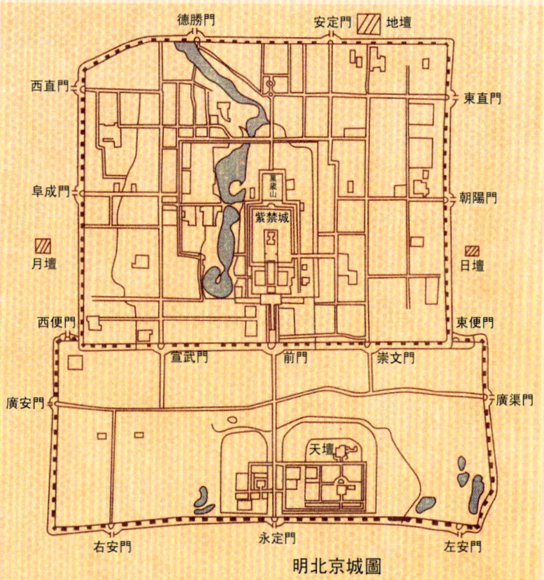

明北京城圖

妙語如珠 Words & Phrases

yí rì zhī jì zài yú chén yì nián zhī jì zài yú chūn

一日之計在於晨，一年之計在於春。

計 here means "key time." Morning hours are the best time to do a day's work. A year's work depends on a good start in the Spring.

◆例句：

"一日之計在於晨"，許多學生喜歡在早上跑步，呼吸新鮮空氣。"一年之計在於春"，小明在新學期開始的時候，就定好了學習中文的計劃。

◆生字詞

學期	xué qī	term, semester, school term
新鮮	xīn xiān	fresh
空氣	kōng qì	air

認讀字詞 Vocabulary

它們	tā men	[plural form of it]
哪裡	nǎ lǐ	where; wherever, all over
下面	xià miàn	under, below
裡面	lǐ miàn	inside
外面	wài miàn	outside
上面	shàng miàn	on top of, above
前面	qián miàn	in front of
後面	hòu miàn	behind
西瓜	xī guā	watermelon
冰箱	bīng xiāng	refrigerator
老鼠	lǎo shǔ	mouse, rat
電腦	diàn nǎo	computer

學寫字 Writing

Write the following characters.

後 hòu back

後

面 miàn side

面

外 wài outside

外

鼠 shǔ mouse, rat

鼠

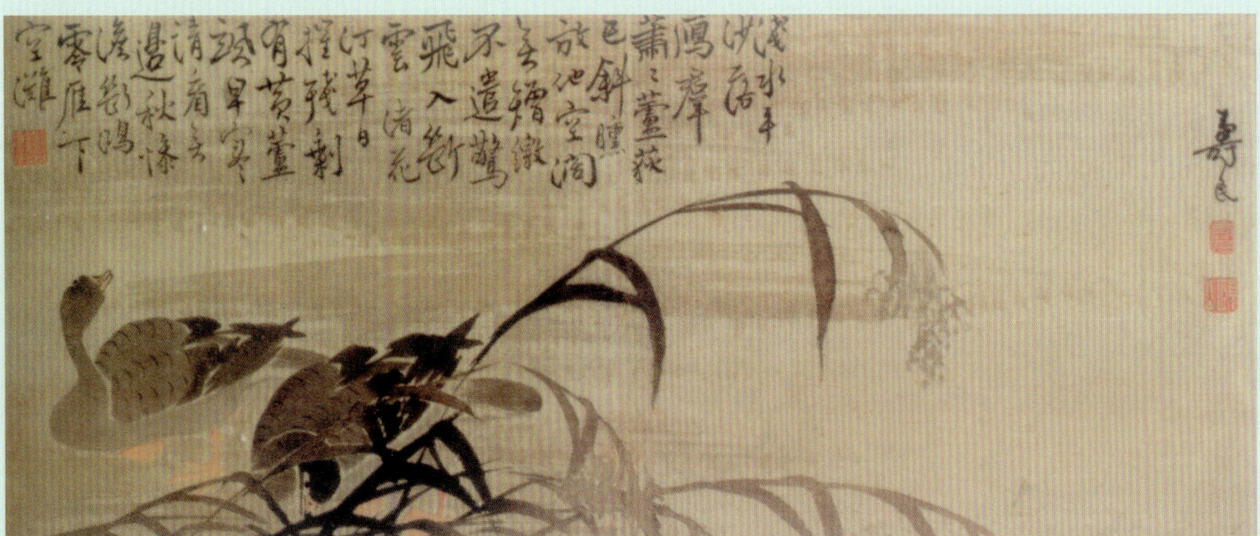

蘆雁圖冊（一） 清朝（1616—1911） 邊壽民

Qing Dynasty painting, by Bian Shou-min

第二十六課 她的爸爸做什麼工作？

zuò gōngzuò

第二十六課　她的爸爸做什麼工作？

課 文 Text

王小文的媽媽做(zuò)什麼工作(gōngzuò)？

她的媽媽是商(shāng)人。

王小文的爸爸做什麼工作？

她的爸爸是老師。

王小文的爺爺(yéye)做什麼工作？

她的爺爺是醫生(yīshēng)。

王小文的奶奶(nǎinai)做什麼工作？

她的奶奶是家庭(jiātíng)主婦(zhǔfù)。

王小文是中學生(zhōngxuéshēng)還(hái)是小學生？

她是中學生。

王小文的弟弟也是中學生嗎？

不，他不是中學生。他是小學生。

語　法 Grammar

做什麼工作？

When asking what someone's occupation is, one can say 你做什麼工作？ To answer the question, replace 什麼 with the type of work.

你的爸爸做什麼工作？ What does your dad do for a living?	我的爸爸是商人。 My dad is a businessman.
你做什麼工作？ What do you do for a living?	我沒有工作，我是學生。 I don't have a job, I am a student.
你的媽媽做什麼工作？ What does your mom do for a living?	我的媽媽是醫生。 My mom is a doctor.
她的媽媽做什麼工作？ What does her mom do for a living?	她的媽媽是老師。 Her mom is a teacher.

是…還是…

是 and 還是 combine to pose a question that includes an alternative.

王小文的弟弟是中學生還是小學生？
Is WANG Xiaowen's brother a secondary school student or an elementary school student?

到下一個路口是左轉還是右轉？
Do we turn left or turn right at the next intersection?

你想吃香蕉還是葡萄？
Do you want bananas or grapes?

明天會颳風還是會下雨？
Will it be windy or rainy tomorrow?

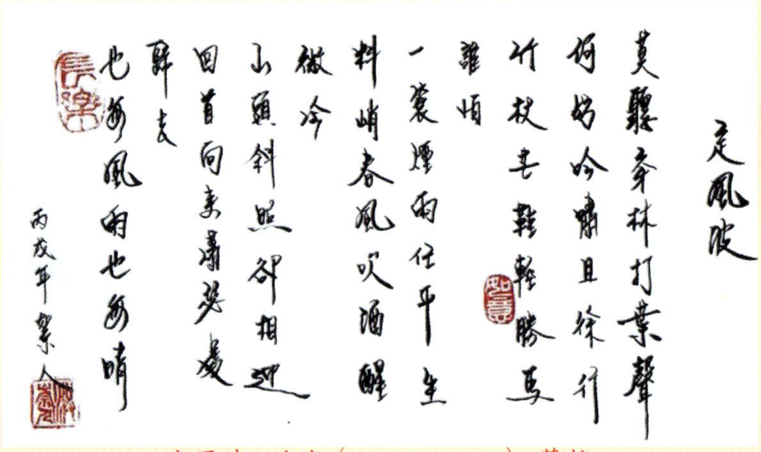

定風波　北宋（960—1127）蘇軾
Poem in the Ding-Feng-Bo style by Su Shi, Northern Sung Dynasty

句型練習 Exercises

她的哥哥是中學生嗎？

你媽媽、醫生⇨ ______________________________？

白大衛的爸爸、商人⇨ ______________________________？

她、老師⇨ ______________________________？

你的小狗、黃色的⇨ ______________________________？

她的爸爸做什麼工作？

她的媽媽、穿、衣服⇨ ______________________________？

你、喜歡、運動⇨ ______________________________？

李校長、開、車⇨ ______________________________？

今天奶奶、做、飯⇨ ______________________________？

你想吃香蕉還是葡萄？

你的爸爸是商人、醫生

⇨ ______________________________？

你喜歡打籃球、打乒乓球

⇨ ______________________________？

我今天穿短褲上學、穿裙子上學

⇨ ______________________________？

試試看 Challenge

王小文家有六個人。他們是爺爺、奶奶、爸爸、媽媽、弟弟和她。他們住在大華路。

她的爺爺是醫生。她的奶奶是家庭主婦。她的爸爸是商人。她的媽媽是老師。她上九年級，是中學生。她的弟弟上四年級，是小學生。

她的爸爸喜歡跑步。她的媽媽喜歡打網球。她的弟弟喜歡打籃球。小文喜歡游泳。小文的爺爺和奶奶喜歡打太極拳。

◆生字詞

太極拳	tài jí quán	Tai Chi, shadow boxing

讀一讀 Reading

將來做什麼？

A：白大衛　B：李大中　C：白瑪麗

A：你將來想做什麼？
B：我要做一個運動員。
C：你想做什麼樣的運動員？
B：我喜歡打籃球，希望將來成為職業球員。你呢？
C：我想做一個演員。
A：哇！真酷！你要演什麼？
C：我要演灰姑娘，和我的白馬王子一起跳舞！
B：大衛，你呢？
A：我將來要做警察。“站住！舉起手來！”
B、C：哈哈！

◆生字詞

將來	jiāng lái	in the future
運動員	yùn dòng yuán	athlete

職業	zhí yè	profession, professional
演員	yǎn yuán	actor
酷	kù	awesome, cool
灰姑娘	huī gū niang	Cinderella's Chinese name
白馬王子	bái mǎ wáng zǐ	"Prince on a white horse" (Prince Charming)
一起	yì qǐ	together
跳舞	tiào wǔ	to dance
警察	jǐng chá	policeman
站住，舉起手來！	zhàn zhù, jǔ qǐ shǒu lái !	Stop! Hands up!

Discovering China

文化

China's Shadow Puppet Theater 皮影戲

China has an interesting type of traditional theater called *Pi Ying Xi* (皮影戲), which translates literally to "Leather Shadow Play." This name reflects the fact that performers use puppets made out of leather or paper to tell a story. During the performance, the silhouettes of the puppets are cast onto a screen by lights, while performers behind the stage operate the puppets and sing at the same time, accompanied by music. Because it is such fun to watch, shadow puppet theater has always been very popular in China.

妙語如珠 Words & Phrases

shú néng shēng qiǎo
熟能生巧

Skill comes from practice; practice makes perfect.

例句：
瑪麗的中文説得很好，同學們問她原因，她説："熟能生巧，多聽多説自然就會了。"

生字詞

原因	yuán yīn	reason
自然	zì rán	naturally; of course; nature

認讀字詞 Vocabulary

做	zuò	to do, work
工作	gōng zuò	work, job
商人	shāng rén	businessperson
爺爺	yé ye	grandfather (paternal)
醫生	yī shēng	doctor
奶奶	nǎi nai	grandmother (paternal)
家庭主婦	jiā tíng zhǔ fù	homemaker
中學	zhōng xué	secondary school
還是	hái shì	or
中學生	zhōng xué shēng	secondary school student
小學生	xiǎo xué shēng	elementary school student

學寫字 Writing

Write the following characters.

商 shāng business

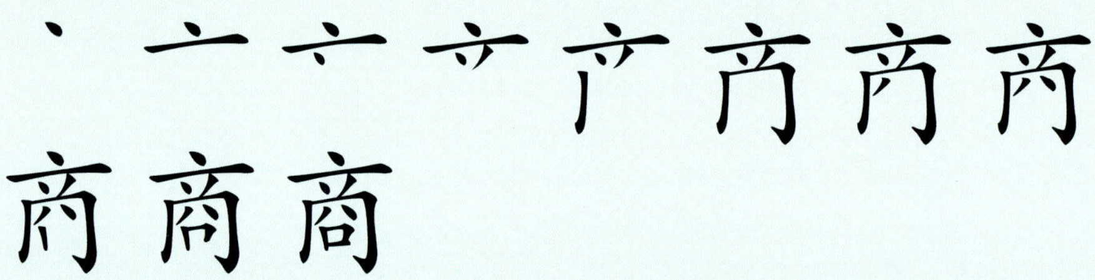

醫 yī to cure

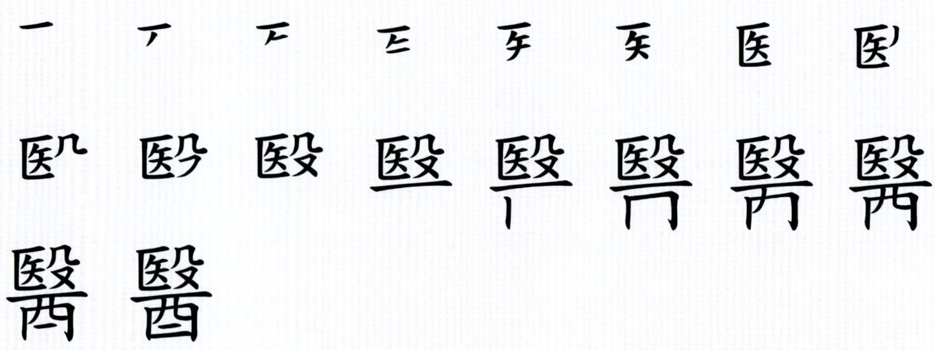

學 xué to study, learn

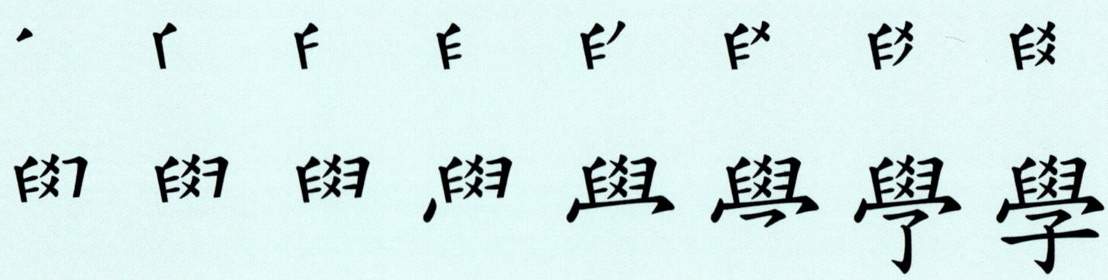

故宮裡的香爐
An incense burner in the Forbidden City

第二十七課　我的一天

xiàn diǎn
現在幾點了？
現在六點了。
現在幾點了？
bàn
現在八點半了。
現在幾點了？
fēn
現在兩點十五分了。
現在幾點了？
現在三點五分了。

第二十七課　我的一天

zǎo　　qǐchuáng
你早上幾點起床？
我早上六點半起床。
zǎofàn
你幾點吃早飯？
我七點吃早飯。
你幾點上學？
我七點四十五分上學。

第二十七課　我的一天

fàng
你幾點放學？
我下午三點二十分放學。
gōngkè
你幾點做功課？
我下午四點半做功課。
wǎn shuìjiào
你晚上幾點睡覺？
我晚上十點睡覺。

課文 Text

Xiàn diǎn
現在幾點了？現在六點了。

bàn
現在幾點了？現在八點半了。

fēn
現在幾點了？現在兩點十五分了。

現在幾點了？現在三點五分了。

zǎo qǐchuáng
你早上幾點起床？

我早上六點半起床。

zǎofàn
你幾點吃早飯？

我七點吃早飯。

你幾點上學？

我七點四十五分上學。

fàng
你幾點放學？

我下午三點二十分放學。

gōngkè
你幾點做功課？

我下午四點半做功課。

wǎn shuìjiào
你晚上幾點睡覺？

我晚上十點睡覺。

語法 Grammar

幾點

幾點 means "what time?"

你早上幾點起床？ What time do you get up in the morning?	我早上六點半起床。 I get up at 6:30 in the morning.
你哥哥幾點吃早飯？ What time does your brother eat breakfast?	我哥哥七點十五分吃早飯。 My brother eats breakfast at 7:15 in the morning.
李小姐晚上幾點睡覺？ What time does Miss LI go to sleep?	她晚上十點睡覺。 She goes to sleep at 10:00 at night.

句型練習 Exercises

現在是下午三點。

晚上、九點二十分 ⇨ ____________________。

上午、十一點十分 ⇨ ____________________。

中午、十二點 ⇨ ____________________。

下午、兩點半 ⇨ ____________________。

你七點起床嗎？

王老師、八點、上課⇨ ______________________ ？

你媽媽、六點、做早飯⇨ ______________________ ？

她、三點半、放學⇨ ______________________ ？

王小文、十點半、睡覺⇨ ______________________ ？

早上六點半媽媽叫我起床。

中午十二點、奶奶、吃飯⇨ ______________________ 。

星期天、李校長、去學校⇨ ______________________ 。

放學後、白大衛、打籃球⇨ ______________________ 。

晚上七點、媽媽、做功課⇨ ______________________ 。

試試看 Challenge

每天早上六點媽媽叫我起床。吃完早飯，七點半我坐校車去上學。中午十二點我在學校吃午飯。下午三點二十分放學。放學後，我在學校裡打球。五點回家做功課。晚上七點和家人一起吃晚飯。晚飯後，我們一起看書。我每天晚上十點睡覺。

現在幾點？（兒歌"Frere Jacques"調）

現在幾點？現在幾點？

下午三點，下午三點。三點要做什麼？

三點要回家了。誰的家？我的家。

◆生字詞

完	wán	to finish
每	měi	every
回	huí	back, return

讀一讀 Reading

謎語

兩隻手，一長一短，

一天到晚跑不停，

一個快一個慢，

太陽正中，手在一起。（打一物）

傳統計時器—日晷(rì guǐ)
A traditional time-telling instrument—a sun dial

◆生字詞

謎語	mí yǔ	riddle
停	tíng	to stop
太陽	tài yáng	the sun
正中	zhèng zhōng	right in the middle
打一物	dǎ yí wù	take a guess (only used for riddles)

Discovering China

文化

Walking Birds 遛鳥

A lot of Beijing people "walk birds" as a hobby. This is an age-old custom. What does it mean to walk a bird? If you visit a park or a wooded area in Beijing in the early morning, you will see a lot of people there, mostly elderly, strolling around leisurely while holding a bird cage, or perhaps carrying a bamboo pole on their shoulders with two bird cages hanging from each end. Many old folks enjoy gathering together, showing off their birds, and chatting with each other about their bird-raising experiences. When they get tired of carrying the cages, they'll hang them on a branch and sit together under the trees. They chat about current events, breathe the fresh air, and listen to the pleasant sounds of the birds singing. Walking birds is a relaxing and pleasant activity that Beijingers really enjoy.

街頭雕塑—遛鳥
Street sculpture — Walking Birds

妙語如珠 Words & Phrases

yì tiān dào wǎn
一天到晚

All the time; all day long.

◆例句：
他什麼事都不做，一天到晚玩電子遊戲。

認讀字詞 Vocabulary

現在	xiàn zài	now
點	diǎn	point; o'clock
半	bàn	half
分	fēn	minute
早上	zǎo shàng	morning
起床	qǐ chuáng	to get out of bed
早飯	zǎo fàn	breakfast
放學	fàng xué	school dismissal
功課	gōng kè	homework
做功課	zuò gōng kè	to do homework
睡覺	shuì jiào	to sleep

學寫字 Writing

Write the following characters.

現 xiàn present

一 二 干 王 玎 玑 玥 玥 珇 現 現

分 fēn minute

丿 八 今 分

早 zǎo early

丨 冂 日 日 旦 早

半 bàn half, in the middle

丶 丷 丷 兰 半

第二十八課　這是誰的房間？

課文 Text

這是誰的房間(fángjiān)？這是我的房間。我的房間很大。它是藍色的。

房間裡有床(chuáng)、沙發(shāfā)、桌子、椅子、書架(jià)和衣櫃(guì)。床上有棒球帽(bàngqiúmào)和雜誌(zázhì)。桌子上有電腦和手機(shǒujī)。書架上有很多中文書和英文書。我喜歡在房間裡玩(wán)電腦，也喜歡在房間裡看(kàn)書和寫字。

我很喜歡我的房間。

房 房 房 房 房

語 法 Grammar

有什麼？

有什麼？means "to have what?"

房間裡有什麼？ What is there in the room?	房間裡有床、沙發、桌子、椅子、書架和衣櫃。 There is a bed, a sofa, a desk, a chair, a bookshelf and a closet in the room.
桌子上有什麼？ What is on the desk?	桌子上有電腦和筆。 There is a computer and some pens on the desk.
椅子上有什麼？ What is on the chair?	椅子上有玩具(wán jù)。 There are toys on the chair.
書架上有什麼？ What is on the bookshelf?	書架上有很多書。 There are many books on the bookshelf.

句 型 練 習 Exercises

這是誰的房間？

那、書架 ⇨ ______________________ ？

他們、學生 ⇨ ______________________ ？

王小文、姊姊 ⇨ ______________________ ？

那、筆 ⇨ ______________________ ？

房間裡有床嗎？

椅子、上、書 ⇨ ______________________ ？

電腦、前面、蘋果 ⇨ ______________________ ？

學校、外面、公園 ⇨ ______________________ ？

衣櫃、裡、衣服 ⇨ ______________________ ？

桌子上有電腦和筆。

書架上、法文書、英文書⇨ ______________________________。

衣櫃裡、衣服、鞋⇨ ______________________________。

教室裡、白板、桌子⇨ ______________________________。

房間裡、床、沙發⇨ ______________________________。

試 試 看 Challenge

那是我弟弟的房間。我弟弟的房間不大。他的房間是綠色的。房間裡有床、沙發、桌子、椅子、書架和衣櫃。可是，他的房間裡沒有很多玩具。弟弟現在不喜歡玩具，他喜歡玩電腦、打籃球。他的書架上有書，還有很多DVD、兩個籃球和一個足球。房間的牆上有很多籃球明星的大海報。

◆生字詞

玩具	wán jù	toys
牆	qiáng	wall
明星	míng xīng	celebrities, stars
海報	hǎi bào	poster

讀一讀 Reading

我的房間裡有一張姚明的海報。姚明是籃球運動員，中國上海人。他的生日是1980年9月12日，屬猴，身高七尺多。姚明最喜歡的顏色是藍色，他喜歡玩電腦遊戲、上網和看書。他在球場上打中鋒。姚明22歲的時候去美國NBA打球。

生字詞

張	zhāng	piece [a measure word for paper]
姚明	yáo míng	a famous basketall player
上海	shàng hǎi	Shanghai
屬	shǔ	belong to (zodiac sign)
尺	chǐ	foot, feet [measurement only]
遊戲	yóu xì	game
上網	shàng wǎng	go online
球場	qiú chǎng	ball court
中鋒	zhōng fēng	center (position in basketball)
隊	duì	team

Discovering China

文化

Multi-Generational Chinese Households 大家庭

In traditional Chinese society, the ideal household has always been multi-generational: several generations of people (parents, children, grandchildren) all living together. It was many people's ideal to have a large family with many grandchildren, and it was common to have three or even four or five generations of a family living together. But in today's society, because people tend to wait until they are older to get married, it is very rare to see a four-generation household anymore in China. Also, due to family planning policies, the majority of families have only one child. However, there are still many households in China with three generations under one roof. In these families, adults with a child will continue to live with their parents. This way, the older generation will not get lonely, and young children will have someone to look after them while their parents are working. Many Chinese people feel that this system makes life easier for everyone in the family.

妙 語 如 珠 Words & Phrases

mǎ dào chéng gōng

馬 到 成 功

Succeed on first try.

◆例句：

你明天就要考試了，祝你馬到成功，得到理想的分數。

◆生字詞

分數	fēn shù	score
理想	lǐ xiǎng	ideal, desirable, desired

認 讀 字 詞 Vocabulary

房間	fáng jiān	room
床	chuáng	bed
沙發	shā fā	sofa
書架	shū jià	bookshelf
衣櫃	yī guì	closet (for clothing)
棒球	bàng qiú	baseball
帽	mào	cap, hat
雜誌	zá zhì	magazine
手機	shǒu jī	cell phone, mobile phone
很多	hěn duō	very many
玩	wán	to play
玩電腦	wán diàn nǎo	to play on the computer
看書	kàn shū	to read a book

學寫字 Writing

Write the following characters.

看 kàn to look, see

一 二 三 手 手 看 看 看 看

玩 wán to play

一 二 干 王 玎 玗 玩 玩

寫 xiě to write

丶 丷 宀 宀 宀 宀 宀 宀 宀 宀 寫 寫 寫 寫 寫

帽 mào cap, hat

丨 冂 巾 巾 帄 帄 帽 帽 帽 帽 帽 帽

書五律詩　清朝（1616—1911）張在辛
Shu-Wu style poem by Zhang Zai Xin, Qing Dynasty

第二十九課　他們在做什麼？

第二十九課　他們在做什麼？

課　文 Text

今天是星期天。白大衛的一家人都在家。

爸爸和媽媽在看電視(diànshì)。姊姊和妹妹在看書。弟弟和他的好朋友在一起玩電腦遊戲(yóuxì)。白大衛在做功課。

小狗在做什麼？牠(tā)在啃骨頭(kěngǔtou)。小貓在做什麼？牠在睡覺。

金魚(jīnyú)在做什麼？牠在水裡游來游去。

語 法 Grammar

…做什麼？你（他…）在做什麼？

做什麼？means "what are you doing?" 你在做什麼？To answer, replace 什麼 with the activity. The 在 in the sentence indicates it is an ongoing activity about which you are asking.

弟弟在做什麼？ What is Younger Brother doing?	他在畫畫。 He is drawing.
爺爺在做什麼？ What is Grandpa doing?	他在看書。 He is reading books.
你在做什麼？ What are you doing?	我在做功課。 I am doing homework.
小鳥在做什麼？ What is the little bird doing?	牠在飛來飛去。 It is flying around.

句型練習 Exercises

弟弟在畫畫嗎？

小貓、睡覺⇨ ______________________________ ?

白瑪麗、做功課⇨ ______________________________ ?

她們、聽音樂⇨ ______________________________ ?

王小文和妹妹、看電視⇨ ______________________________ ?

公園裡的人真多！

今天天氣、好⇨ ______________________________ !

你家的小動物、可愛⇨ ______________________________ !

她的裙子、好看⇨ ______________________________ !

她的眼睛、大⇨ ______________________________ !

小鳥在天上飛來飛去。

小魚、水裡、游⇨ ____________________。

弟弟、房間裡、跑⇨ ____________________。

李校長、教室外面、走⇨ ____________________。

試試看 Challenge

今天上午我去公園玩。

公園裡的人真多呀！我看到了王小文、李大中、白大衛和白瑪麗。

王小文和白瑪麗在打網球。

李大中和白大衛在打乒乓球。

還有幾個小學生在踢足球。很多老爺爺、老奶奶在散步。

◆生字詞

真	zhēn	really
散步	sàn bù	take a walk

讀一讀 Reading

藍藍的天，紅紅的花，我唱著歌兒騎著馬。什麼馬？大馬。什麼大？天大。什麼天？青天。什麼青？山青。什麼山？高山。什麼高？塔高。什麼塔？寶塔。什麼寶？國寶。什麼國？我國。

◆生字詞

青	qīng	green or blue
塔	tǎ	pagoda
山	shān	mountain
寶	bǎo	treasure

Discovering China

文化

Weekends in Beijing 北京人的週末

In the busy life of the capital city, the weekend is a rare opportunity for rest and relaxation, and is a time to get together with friends and family. Many adults go to visit their parents on the weekend, and the entire family will give each other updates on what's going on in their lives while they all help out in the kitchen to prepare a meal. They often find that a week's worth of weariness is washed away by warm chatter with family members. In some families, children will accompany their parents on shopping trips, followed by a visit to the park, and then a meal at a restaurant. Beijingers find this atmosphere of family togetherness comforting and relaxing.

妙語如珠 Words & Phrases

huān tiān xǐ dì

歡天喜地

With boundless joy; overjoyed.

◆例句：

我們的球隊比賽得了冠軍，大家歡天喜地，慶祝了半天。

國畫—孩子嬉戲

Traditional Chinese painting—Children at play

◆生字詞

半天	bàn tiān	half a day, "a long time" in this context

認讀字詞 Vocabulary

一家人	yì jiā rén	a family
看	kàn	to watch, look at
電視	diàn shì	television
看電視	kàn diàn shì	to watch television
遊戲	yóu xì	game
電腦遊戲	diàn nǎo yóu xì	computer games
牠	tā	it [for animals]
啃骨頭	kěn gǔ tou	to gnaw on a bone
游來游去	yóu lái yóu qù	to swim back and forth
金魚	jīn yú	goldfish
一起	yì qǐ	together

學寫字 Writing

Write the following characters.

電 diàn electricity

一 ㇀ 𠂇 ...

竹石山禽圖 清朝（1616—1911） 陳宇
Mountain Fowl by Chen Yu, Qing Dynasty

diànhuà

第三十課　打電話

第三十課　打電話 (diànhuà)

課　文 Text

A：喂(wèi)！你好！

B：你好！

A：請問李大中在嗎？

B：在，請等(děng)一下。

C：喂！你好！

A：嗨(hāi)！我是王小文。你明天下午有空(kòng)來我家嗎？

C：對(duì)不起，我明天沒空。

A：沒關係(méiguānxi)，那麼(nàme)下星期六上午怎麼樣？

C：好啊。我下星期六上午有空。

A：太好了(tàihǎole)！下星期見！

C：再見！

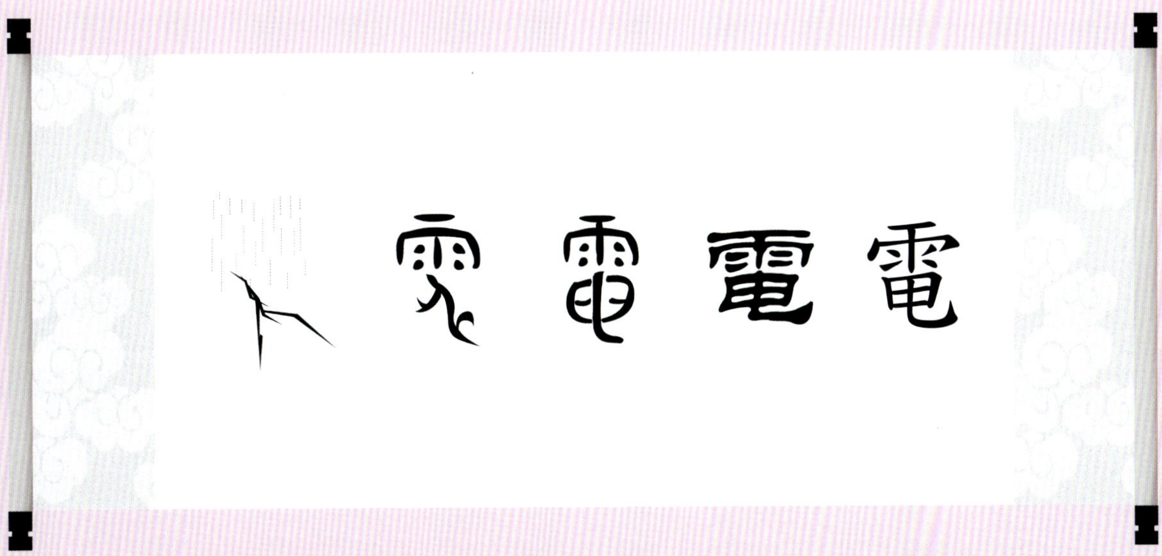

語 法 Grammar

請問

A polite way to start a question.

請問，李大中在家嗎？	May I ask, is LI Dazhong home?
請問，你想吃什麼？	What would you like to eat, please?
請問，去動物園怎麼走？	Can you please tell me how to get to the zoo?

對不起！	sorry; excuse me
沒關係！	no problem, it's okay.

句型練習 Exercises

請你明天下午來我家玩。

我的好朋友、星期天、和我過生日

⇨ ______________________________。

他們、後天晚上、一起吃晚飯

⇨ ______________________________。

小文、明年、去德國玩

⇨ ______________________________。

我給明明和麗麗打電話。

爸爸、我、錢 ⇨ ______________________________。

老師、我們、上課 ⇨ ______________________________。

媽媽、我和妹妹、買了一本書

⇨ ______________________________。

試試看 Challenge

我家買了新房子。我想請我的好朋友到我的新家玩。我給明明和麗麗打電話，請他們下星期六上午來我家。明明説他沒空，因為他的爺爺和奶奶要來北京。他們一家人要去長城和故宮玩。麗麗説她有空，可以來。我很高興，因為我們可以一起游泳，也可以一起玩電腦。

◆生字詞

新	xīn	new
因為	yīn wèi	because
長城	cháng chéng	the Great Wall
故宮	gù gōng	the Forbidden City
高興	gāo xìng	happy

讀一讀 Reading

（Ring Ring Ring...）

小麗的媽媽：喂？

小明：阿姨，您好！請問小麗在嗎？

小麗的媽媽：她不在，請問你是誰？

小明：我是她同學，我叫小明。我想問她今天的數學功課。請她給我回電話好嗎？

小麗的媽媽：好，你的電話號碼是多少？

小明：我的電話是630-555-1234。

小麗的媽媽：小麗回來後，我會告訴她。

小明：謝謝阿姨！

小麗的媽媽：不客氣！再見！

小明：再見！

◆生字詞

阿姨	ā yí	auntie [polite way to address an older woman]
您	nín	you [polite form]
號碼	hào mǎ	number to indicate the order of something in a series
告訴	gào su	to tell

Discovering China

文化

Chinese Musical Instruments: The Zither 古箏 (gǔ zhēng)

The *zheng*, or zither, is one of China's oldest instruments. Because it has been used in China for over 2,000 years, it is also called the *gu-zheng*, the "ancient zither." The earliest known forms of the *gu-zheng*, from the Warring States period (公元前475-公元前221), had five strings and a bamboo body. More strings were gradually added over time; today, the most common type of *gu-zheng* has 21 strings. The *gu-zheng* may be played as a solo instrument, as part of an ensemble, or to accompany a vocal performance. It makes a truly beautiful sound that is considered very pure, elegant, and refined. Because the *gu-zheng* gives the artist so much control over the quality and pitch of the sound, it is rich in expressive power and can convey a wide range of emotions.

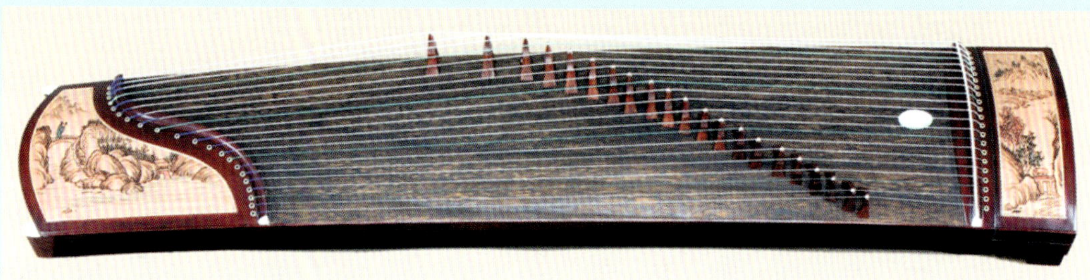

古箏
A Chinese Zither

妙語如珠 Words & Phrases

fèi huà lián piān 廢話連篇	méi wán méi liǎo 沒完沒了
Full of nonsense. ◆例句： 大文喜歡打電話，但是講起話來廢話連篇。	Incessant, continuous, without end. ◆例句： 大文和小衛打起電話來總是沒完沒了，常常一講就是幾十分鐘。

認讀字詞 Vocabulary

嗨	hāi	hi
喂	wèi	hello? [on the phone]

電話	diàn huà	telephone
打電話	dǎ diàn huà	to make a phone call
在家	zài jiā	at home
等一下	děng yí xià	wait a minute
沒空	méi kòng	not available, no time
對不起	duì bù qǐ	sorry
沒關係	méi guān xi	it doesn't matter, it's okay, no problem
太好了！	tài hǎo le	that's great!
那麼	nà me	then
下	xià	next

學寫字 Writing

Write the following characters.

等 děng to wait

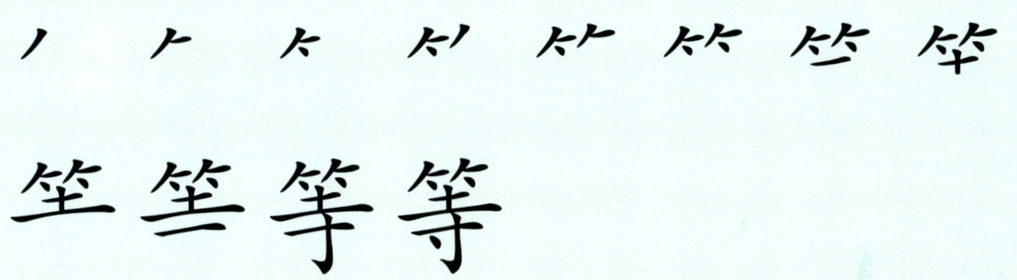

空 kòng empty

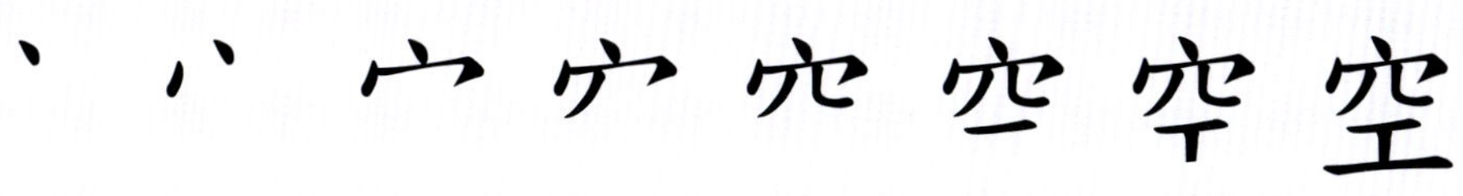

對 duì to match; correct

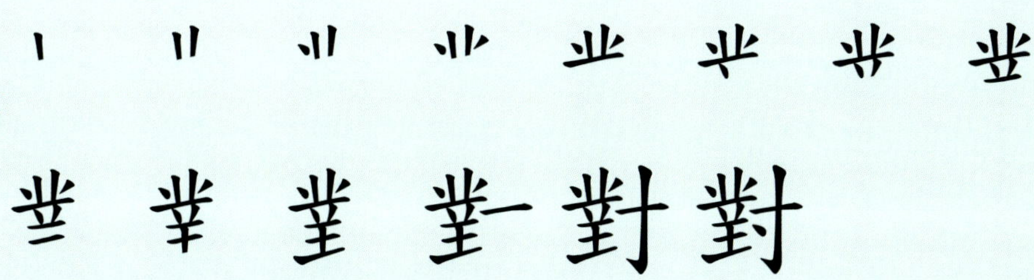

話 huà word

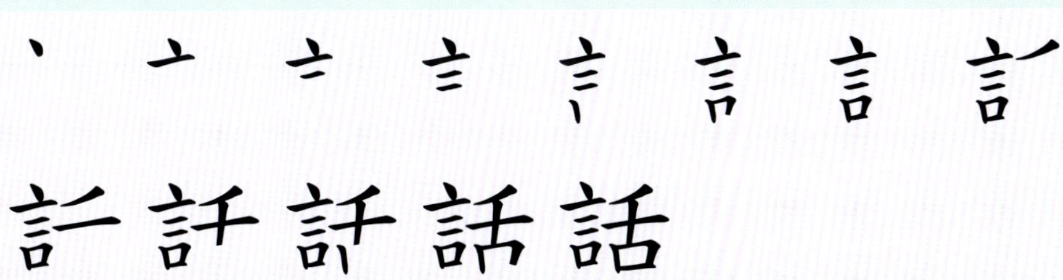

第三十一課　你今天上了什麼課？

課文 Text

	星期一	星期二	星期三	星期四	星期五
8:10 – 9:00	英文	數學	英文	數學	英文
9:10 – 10:00	英文	數學	英文	數學	生物
10:10 – 11:00	歷史	物理	歷史	物理	生物
11:10 –12:00	數學	中文	數學	中文	音樂
12:00 – 1:00	午餐	午餐	午餐	午餐	午餐
1:10 – 2:00	生物	歷史	生物	歷史	電腦
2:10 – 3:00	中文	體育	中文	體育	電腦

A: 你今天上了什麼課(kè)？

B: 今天是星期三。我上午有英文，歷史(lìshǐ)，數學(shùxué)。

下午上了生物(shēngwù)和中文。

A: 你每天(měitiān)的課都不一樣(yàng)嗎？

B: 對，我一、三的課一樣，二、四的課一樣，但星期五的課不太一樣。

B: 你每天的課一樣嗎？

A: 我每天的課也不太一樣。

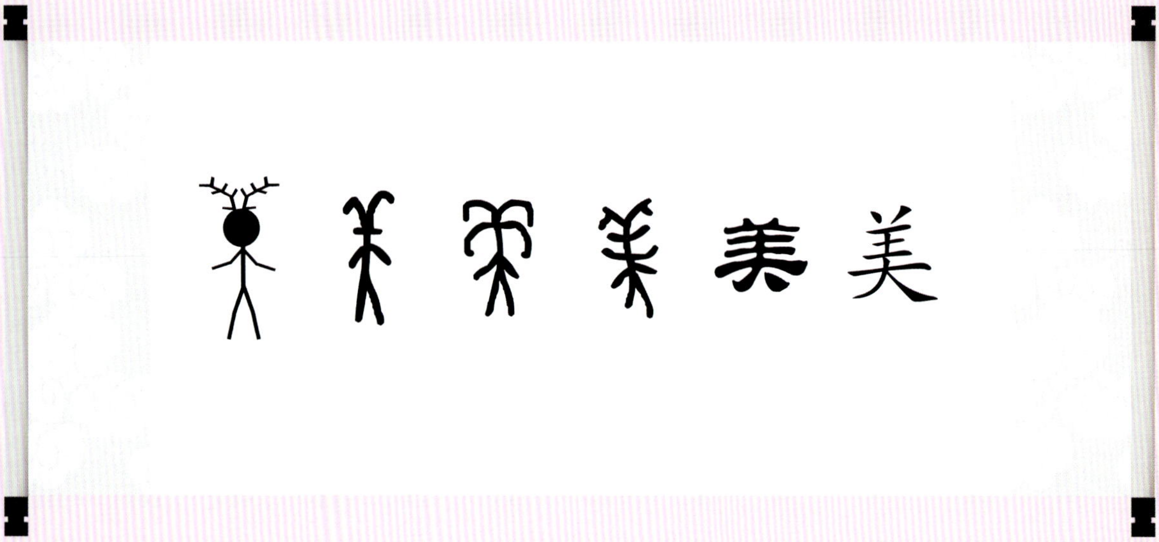

語 法 Grammar

都不一樣

都不一樣 means they are all different.

你每天的課都不一樣嗎？
Do you have different classes everyday?

每天的天氣都不一樣嗎？
Is the weather different everyday?

他家每個房間都不一樣嗎？
Is each room in his house different?

句 型 練 習 Exercises

你今天上了什麼課？

上個星期、讀、書⇨ ______________________________ ？

昨天、買、衣服⇨ ______________________________ ？

剛才、吃、水果⇨ ______________________________ ？

中午、吃、飯⇨ ______________________________ ？

從星期一到星期五我都上學。

五年前、現在、喜歡踢足球

⇨ ____。

三點、七點、沒空

⇨ ____。

今天晚上、明天上午、在飛機上

⇨ ____。

每個房間都不太一樣。

今天天氣、好

⇨ ____。

這條裙子、好看

⇨ ____。

我和王小文都、喜歡跑步

⇨ ____。

白大衛和李大中都、高

⇨ ____。

蘆雁圖冊（二） 清朝（1616—1911） 邊壽民
Qing Dynasty painting, by Bian Shou-min

試試看 Challenge

從星期一到星期五我都上學。我每天的課都不太一樣。今天是星期四,我上午有數學、科學、閱讀、寫作和電腦，下午有社會學、美術、體育和外語。我選的外語是中文。我最喜歡上電腦課，因為電腦課沒有功課。我也很喜歡我的電腦老師，她不高也不矮，不胖也不瘦。她天天穿好看的衣服。

◆生字詞

從	cóng	from
選	xuǎn	to select, choose
科學	kē xué	science
閱讀	yuè dú	reading; to read
寫作	xiě zuò	writing
社會學	shè huì xué	social studies
美術	měi shù	art

讀一讀 Reading

數學課，學數字，七六五四三二一；
美術課，學畫畫，紅橙黃綠青藍紫；
體育課，做運動，天天練出好身體；
音樂課，學唱歌，Do，Re，Mi，Fa，So，La，Ti。
唱首好歌真歡喜。

◆生字詞

畫畫	huà huà	to draw
橙	chéng	orange
紫	zǐ	purple
練	liàn	to practice, train
首	shǒu	[a measure word for songs]
歡喜	huān xǐ	happy

Discovering China

文化

China's curriculum

In China, all middle and high school students have three required courses: Chinese, math, and foreign languages. No matter what the school or program, these three "core courses" are considered the most important and meet most frequently. Many students spend the majority of their time and effort studying for these three classes. In high school, besides these required classes, students in the liberal arts track and students in the science track take additional courses. Liberal arts students take classes on subjects such as history, politics, and geography, while science students study subjects such as physics and chemistry.

妙語如珠 Words & Phrases

xué yǐ zhì yòng
學以致用

Study for the purpose of practical use; study something in order to apply it.

◆例句：

剛剛學了"馬到成功"這個詞語，瑪麗就用它祝福同學，真是學以致用。

國畫—秋實
Traditional Chinese Painting—Autumn Fruit

◆生字詞

祝福	zhù fú	blessing, well wishing

認讀字詞 Vocabulary

課	kè	class
課程	kè chéng	curriculum, course
表	biǎo	table/form, schedule
課程表	kè chéng biǎo	class schedule
上	shàng	to take; to get on

數學	shù xué	mathematics
歷史	lì shǐ	history
生物	shēng wù	biology
午餐	wǔ cān	lunch
物理	wù lǐ	physics
音樂	yīn yuè	music
體育	tǐ yù	physical education
每天	měi tiān	every day
一樣	yí yàng	the same, alike
不太一樣	bú tài yí yàng	not exactly the same

學寫字 Writing

Write the following characters.

數 shù number

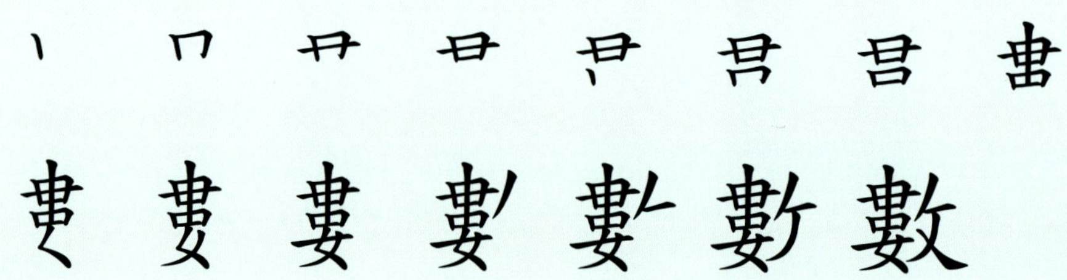

英 yīng English

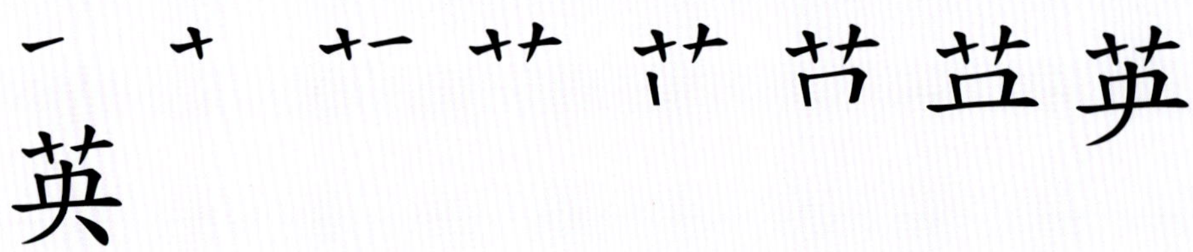

每 měi every

第三十二課　我用(yòng)眼睛看

第三十二課　我用(yòng)眼睛看

課　文 Text

yòng
看什麼？看顏色。怎麼看？我用眼睛看一看。

wén　wèi
聞什麼？聞香味。怎麼聞？我用鼻子聞一聞。

gùshi
說什麼？說故事。怎麼說？我用嘴巴說一說。

yǎo　yáchǐ
咬什麼？咬蘋果。怎麼咬？我用牙齒咬一咬。

tīng　yīnyuè
聽什麼？聽音樂。怎麼聽？我用耳朵聽一聽。

pāi　shuāngshǒu
拍什麼？拍皮球。怎麼拍？我用雙手拍一拍。

shuāng jiǎo mànmàn
走到哪兒？走到公園。怎麼走？我用雙腳慢慢走。

語法 Grammar

用

用 means "use"

我用鼻子聞。
I use my nose to smell.

我用牙齒咬。
I use my teeth to bite.

我用手拍。
I use my hands to clap.

我用嘴巴說。
I use my mouth to speak.

我用耳朵聽。
I use my ears to hear.

我用腳走。
I use my feet to walk.

句型練習 Exercises

你用鼻子聞什麼？

嘴巴、說 ⇨ ______________________ ？

鉛筆、寫 ⇨ ______________________ ？

眼睛、看 ⇨ ______________________ ？

耳朵、聽 ⇨ ______________________ ？

我用雙手拍一拍。

雙腳、跳 ⇨ ______________________ 。

眼睛、看 ⇨ ______________________ 。

嘴巴、嚐 ⇨ ______________________ 。

鼻子、聞 ⇨ ______________________ 。

耳朵、聽 ⇨ ______________________ 。

牠先用鼻子聞一聞，再用牙齒咬一咬。

媽媽、看電視、去買東西⇨ ________________________。

我、做功課、玩遊戲⇨ ________________________。

王小文、游泳、打乒乓球⇨ ________________________。

弟弟、吃飯、吃冰淇淋⇨ ________________________。

試試看 Challenge

我家的小狗叫可可。牠今年四歲。牠是一隻花狗，有白色和咖啡色的毛。牠的眼睛很大，很可愛。

我放學回家，牠喜歡用鼻子聞我，還喜歡用腳拍我，要我給牠東西吃。我給牠一塊木頭，牠先用鼻子聞一聞，再用牙齒咬一咬，可是牠不吃。

我一拍手，可可的耳朵就會豎起來，牠的一雙前腳也會豎起來。我很喜歡和牠玩。

◆生字詞

毛	máo	fur
先	xiān	first
豎	shù	upright

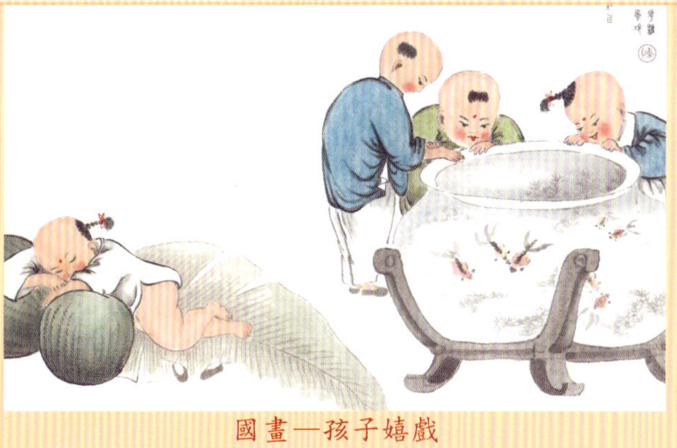

國畫—孩子嬉戲
Traditional Chinese Painting—Children at play

讀一讀 Reading

盲人摸象

幾個盲人不知道大象長的什麼樣子。摸到大象耳朵的人說："大象是一把扇子。"摸到大象腿的人說："大象是一根柱子。"摸到大象身體的人說："大象是一面牆。"摸到大象尾巴的人說："大象是一根繩子。"大家開始爭吵起來。這個寓言的意思是說，人往往會片面看事情，只看到事情的一部分，自以為完全知道了。

◆生字詞

盲	máng	blind
摸	mō	to feel, stroke, touch
把	bǎ	[a measure word for objects with handles]
扇子	shàn zi	fan
腿	tuǐ	leg
根	gēn	[a measure word for long, slim objects]
柱	zhù	post, upright, pillar
繩子	shéng zi	rope
知道	zhī dào	to know
爭吵	zhēng chǎo	to quarrel
寓言	yù yán	fable
片面	piàn miàn	one-sided, biased

Discovering China

文化

The Dai people (傣族) are one of the 55 officially recognized minority nationalities (少數民族) of China. They have a long-recorded history and a distinct culture that still flourishes to this day. The Dai mostly live in close-knit communities in Yunnan Province. They have a great reverence for water, believing in its cleansing power. They magnify and reflect that power by placing mirrors over their wells. At the Water Splashing Festival (潑水節) that takes place during the Dai New Year, they pour water on each other to wash away the sins of the previous year and prepare for the year ahead.

妙語如珠 Words & Phrases

yí gè bā zhang pāi bù xiǎng

一個巴掌拍不響

One hand alone cannot clap; it takes two to tango.

◆例句：

兩個人因為小事互相爭吵，都說是對方的錯，其實一個巴掌拍不響，雙方都有責任。

◆生字詞

對方	duì fāng	counterpart; opposite side, other side
雙方	shuāng fāng	both sides, two parties
責任	zé rèn	duty, responsibility, obligation

認讀字詞 Vocabulary

用	yòng	to use
聞	wén	to smell
香味	xiāng wèi	sweet smell, fragrance
故事	gù shi	story
咬	yǎo	to bite
牙齒	yá chǐ	tooth, teeth
聽音樂	tīng yīn yuè	listen to music
拍	pāi	to clap
皮球	pí qiú	leather ball, rubber ball
雙	shuāng	two, double, a pair
腳	jiǎo	foot
手	shǒu	hand
慢慢	màn màn	slowly

學寫字 Writing

Write the following characters.

用	yòng to use	丿 冂 月 月 用
拍	pāi to clap	一 十 扌 扌 扌 拍 拍 拍
牙	yá tooth	一 二 于 牙
聽	tīng to hear, listen to	一 厂 丌 丌 耳 耳 耳 耳 耳 耳 耳 耳 耳 耳 耳 耳 聽 聽 聽 聽 聽 聽

潑水節

Dai Water Splashing Festival

第三十三課　這是李老師的家

第三十三課　這是李老師的家

課　文 Text

這是李老師的家。

她家有客廳(tīng)、起居(jū)室、飯廳、廚(chú)房和洗(xǐ)衣(yī)房。她家還有三個臥室(wòshì)、一個書房、兩個衛(wèi)生間。

客廳和起居室在房子的最前面。客廳在右邊(biān)，起居室在左邊。飯廳和廚房在客廳的後面。洗衣房和衛生間在房子的最後面。三個臥室也在房子的後面。兩個臥室中間有一個衛生間。主臥室(zhǔwòshì)裡也有一個衛生間。書房在主臥室和起居室的中間。

房子的中間和外面有很多美麗(měilì)的花和樹(shù)。我喜歡李老師的家。

語法 Grammar

在

在 in front of a word indicates the location of the noun; "to be located at."

客廳和起居室在房子的最前面。
The living room and family room are in the very front of the house.

飯廳和廚房在客廳的後面。
The dining room and kitchen are behind the living room.

臥室在房子的左邊。
The bedroom is on the left side of the house.

洗衣房和衛生間在房子的右邊。
The laundry room and bathroom are on the right side of the house.

養心殿西暖閣

有

有 means "to have" and in describing a place means "there are/there is."

兩個臥室的中間有一個衛生間。
There is a bathroom in between the two bedrooms.

房子的中間和外面有很多美麗的花和樹。
There are flowers and trees in the middle of and outside the house.

床上和桌子上有很多玩具。
There are lots of toys on the bed and the desk.

句型練習 Exercises

臥室在房子的左邊嗎？

飯廳、客廳、前面 ⇨ ______________________ ？

王小文、李大中、右邊 ⇨ ______________________ ？

書包、你、桌子上 ⇨ ______________________ ？

衛生間、兩個臥室、中間 ⇨ ______________________ ？

兩個臥室的中間有一個衛生間。

學校、外面、一個公園➪ ________________________________。

冰箱、裡面、五個蘋果➪ ________________________________。

桌子、上面、一隻小貓➪ ________________________________。

試試看 Challenge

客廳裡有兩個沙發，還有花。李老師喜歡在起居室裡看電視。她家的書房裡有很多書，還有電腦。一個臥室裡有電視，一個臥室裡有玩具熊。主臥室的床是藍色的，因為李老師喜歡藍色。

◆生字詞

熊	bear

讀一讀 Reading

留言

麗麗：

爸爸和媽媽去上班了。早飯在飯廳的桌子上。你今天要穿的衣服放在臥室的椅子上。你的書包裡有一個蘋果，午飯後再吃。不要忘了關燈。我們晚上見！祝你今天開心！

愛你的爸爸、媽媽

◆生字詞

留言	message; to leave a message
上班	to go to work
不要	do not; do not want
忘	to forget
關燈	to turn off the light
開心	to be happy

Discovering China

文化

China's Ancient Gardens 中國古典園林

China's ancient botanical gardens are normally divided into two classes: the northern gardens of the imperial family, and the private gardens of the South. The imperial gardens in northern China were built on a very large scale, in a grand and luxurious style. The Summer Palace (頤和園) in Beijing is an example of a botanical garden in this category. The southern private gardens have a more free and flexible layout, and are full of lovely and appealing scenery. If you would like to see some gardens that are representative of this style, you can go to Suzhou (蘇州) and visit the famous gardens there. While there are major differences in the scale and style of northern and southern botanical gardens, they all celebrate the beauty of nature.

妙 語 如 珠 Words & Phrases

ài wū jí wū
愛 屋 及 烏

love me, love my dog.

◆例句：

大中本來討厭小狗，但是他喜歡一個養著小狗的女孩，"愛屋及烏"，大中慢慢對那隻小狗也有了好感。

◆生字詞

養	yǎng	to raise; to provide for
討厭	tǎo yàn	be a pain in the neck, to incur dislike; to dislike
好感	hǎo gǎn	a good feeling, warm feelings

認 讀 字 詞 Vocabulary

房子	fáng zi	house
客廳	kè tīng	living room
起居室	qǐ jū shì	family room
邊	biān	side; edge
主	zhǔ	master, main
臥室	wò shì	bedroom

書房	shū fáng	study
飯廳	fàn tīng	dining room
廚房	chú fáng	kitchen
洗衣房	xǐ yī fáng	laundry room
衛生間	wèi shēng jiān	bathroom
中間	zhōng jiān	middle
花	huā	flower
樹	shù	tree, plant
美麗	měi lì	beautiful

學寫字 Writing

Write the following characters.

房 fáng room

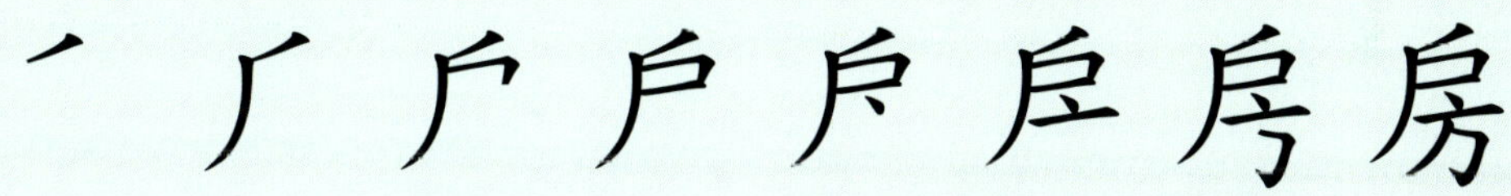

間 jiān room

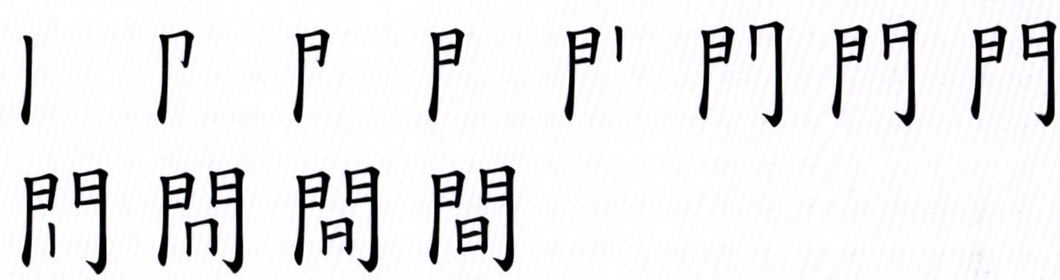

廳 tīng hall

洗 xǐ to wash

美 měi beautiful

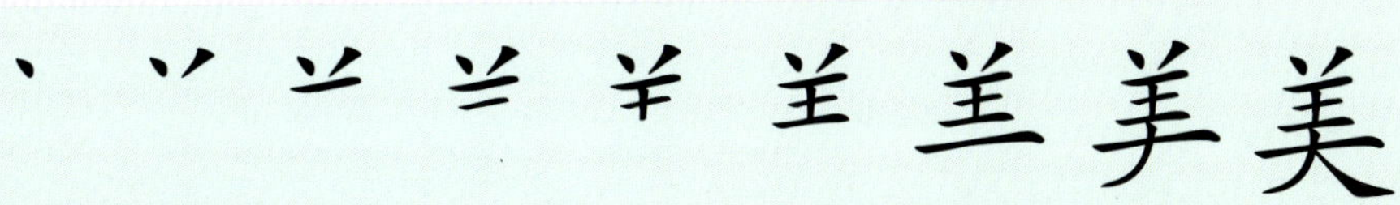

yuán
第三十四課　動物園

yuán

第三十四課　動物園

課文 Text

昨天下午，我和爸爸、媽媽一起去了動物園(yuán)。在動物園裡，我們看見了很多動物，有老(lǎo)虎(hǔ)、獅子(shīzi)、大象、長頸鹿、蛇、袋鼠(dàishǔ)、斑馬(bānmǎ)、猴子，還有大熊貓(xióngmāo)。

我最喜歡大熊貓，因為(yīnwèi)牠又(yòu)可愛又漂亮(piàoliàng)。牠有白色的毛(máo)，黑色的眼睛，小小的耳朵，大大的嘴巴和胖胖的身體，很有趣(yǒuqù)。

語　法 Grammar

一起　together with, in the company of

我和爸爸、媽媽一起去了動物園。
My dad, mom and I went to the zoo together.

弟弟和他的朋友一起玩電腦。
Younger Brother and his friends play on the computer together.

我和同學一起踢足球。
My classmates and I play soccer together.

又…又…

We can use the 又… 又… pattern to talk about something having more than one attribute. The structure is often used like this: 又 + adj + 又 + adj.

牠又可愛又漂亮。
It is cute and also pretty.

王校長又高又瘦。
Principal WANG is tall and slim.

她的貓又白又胖。
Her cat is white and fat.

鳳祥彩繪泥塑-生肖猴

有…還有…

The sentence pattern 有…, 還有… is used to list multiple items. Just as we put "and" before the last item in a list in English ("dogs, cats, and rabbits"), we put 還有 before the final item in a list in Chinese. Their formation is 有 + N, 還有 + N.

我看見了很多動物，有老虎、獅子、大象、長頸鹿、蛇、袋鼠、斑馬、猴子，還有熊貓。
I saw many animals: there were tigers, lions, elephants, giraffes, snakes, kangaroos, zebras, monkeys and also pandas.

我看見了很多人，有校長、老師，還有學生。
I saw a lot of people: the principal, teachers and students.

我看見了很多車，有汽車、火車、自行車，還有出租車。
I saw many vehicles: there were cars, trains, bicycles and taxis.

句型練習 Exercises

大熊貓長什麼樣子？

動物園、有、動物 ⇨ ________________ ？

猴子、吃、水果 ⇨ ________________ ？

你們、玩、遊戲 ⇨ ________________ ？

我和同學一起踢足球。

我、妹妹、洗衣服 ⇨ ________________ 。

哥哥、他的同學、打球 ⇨ ________________ 。

老師、同學們、看書 ⇨ ________________ 。

我、弟弟、看電視 ⇨ ________________ 。

昨天妹妹去了動物園。

去年、哥哥、買、汽車

⇨ ________________ 。

上午、白大衛、看、一本書

⇨ ________________ 。

上星期四、我、看見、王校長

⇨ ________________ 。

試試看 Challenge

今天是星期天，我帶妹妹到動物園玩。動物園裡真熱鬧，有很多老人和孩子，大家來來往往很高興。我們看到了老虎、獅子和大象，還看到了漂亮的大熊貓。妹妹最喜歡孔雀，兩隻美麗的孔雀張開五顏六色的羽毛，向我們展示著牠們的美麗。我最喜歡猴子，小猴子在樹上跳來跳去，真可愛。你喜歡到動物園玩嗎？你喜歡什麼動物？

◆生字詞

熱鬧	rè nao	bustling with activity, lively
來來往往	lái lái wǎng wǎng	coming and going
孔雀	kǒng què	peacock
羽毛	yǔ máo	feather
展示	zhǎn shì	reveal; show

讀一讀 Reading

看看長頸鹿的脖子，像不像一棵樹？
看看袋鼠媽媽的肚子，像不像一個大袋子？
看看大象的鼻子，是不是又長又粗大？
看看斑馬的身體，是不是有白又有黑？
看看大熊貓，是不是又胖又可愛？

◆生字詞

像	xiàng	look like, resemble
肚子	dù zi	stomach
袋子	dài zi	bag, pouch
粗	cū	thick
棵	kē	[a measure word for plants]

小笑話：不良少年

熊貓很喜歡小鹿，可是小鹿拒絕了他，熊貓問：“為什麼呢？”小鹿回答：“我媽媽說了，戴黑眼鏡的都是不良少年。”

斑馬很喜歡猴子，可是猴子拒絕了他，斑馬問：“為什麼呢？”猴子回答：“我媽媽說了，穿花衣服的都是不良少年。”

蜘蛛很喜歡螞蟻，可是螞蟻拒絕了他，蜘蛛問：“為什麼呢？”螞蟻回答：“我媽媽說了，每天在網上待著的都是不良少年。”

◆生字詞

拒絕	jù jué	to refuse
回答	huí dá	answer
戴	dài	wear
眼鏡	yǎn jìng	eyeglasses
不良	bù liáng	not good
少年	shào nián	young adults, teenagers
不良少年	bù liáng shào nián	juvenile delinquent
蜘蛛	zhī zhū	spider
螞蟻	mǎ yǐ	ant
待著	dāi zhe	stay

Discovering China

文化

The Chinese Unicorn 麒麟

The *qilin* (麒麟), or Chinese unicorn, is an animal that appears in ancient Chinese folktales. It has the body of a deer that is covered in fish scales, has a tail, and, of course, has a horn on its head. The status of the unicorn is second only to the dragon in traditional Chinese mythology. In ancient times, Chinese people believed that the unicorn was a lucky animal that would bring you a son and make your family prosperous. For this reason, you can often see the image of a unicorn carved on the roofs of all sorts of buildings. On traditional Chinese clothing, it is common to include a lucky design of "one hundred beasts bowing before the unicorn."

妙 語 如 珠 Words & Phrases

shēng lóng huó hǔ
生 龍 活 虎

Lively as a dragon and energetic as a tiger; brimming with energy.

◆例句：
大文上課時很想睡覺，但是一下課他就變得生龍活虎起來。

jī quǎn bù líng
雞 犬 不 寧

Turmoil in which even fowl and dogs are not left in peace.

◆例句：
樓下的舞廳一直開到深夜，吵鬧的聲音讓附近人家雞犬不寧。

dāi ruò mù jī
呆 若 木 雞

Dumbstruck; to look like a wooden chicken; frightened or shocked to the extent of being unable to speak or move.

◆例句：
第一次看到別人打架，他嚇得呆若木雞，不知道怎麼辦才好。

◆生字詞

舞廳	wǔ tīng	dance hall
一直	yì zhí	always
深夜	shēn yè	late at night
吵鬧	chǎo nào	to disturb
附近	fù jìn	nearby
打架	dǎ jià	fight
嚇得	xià de	afraid

認讀字詞 Vocabulary

看見	kàn jiàn	to see
老虎	lǎo hǔ	tiger
獅子	shī zi	lion
袋鼠	dài shǔ	kangaroo
斑馬	bān mǎ	zebra
大熊貓	dà xióng māo	giant panda
胖胖的	pàng pàng de	chubby, fat
有趣	yǒu qù	interesting
因為	yīn wèi	because
又	yòu	as well, also
漂亮	piào liàng	beautiful, pretty
毛	máo	fur

學寫字 Writing

Write the following characters.

還 hái still

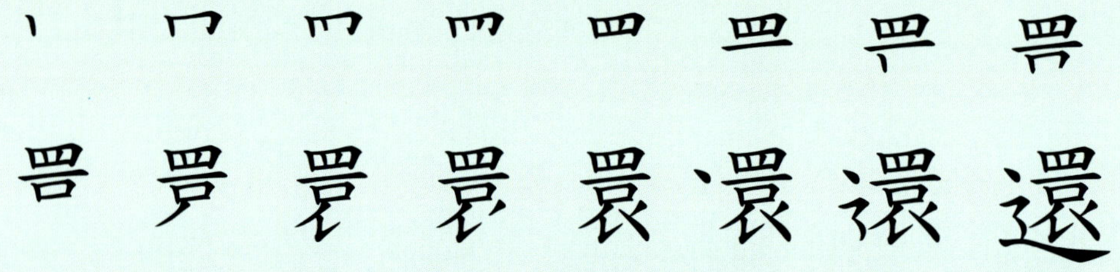

起 qǐ rise

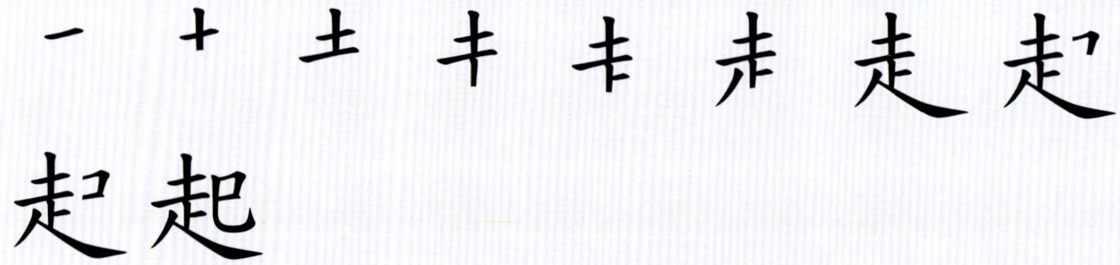

園 yuán garden

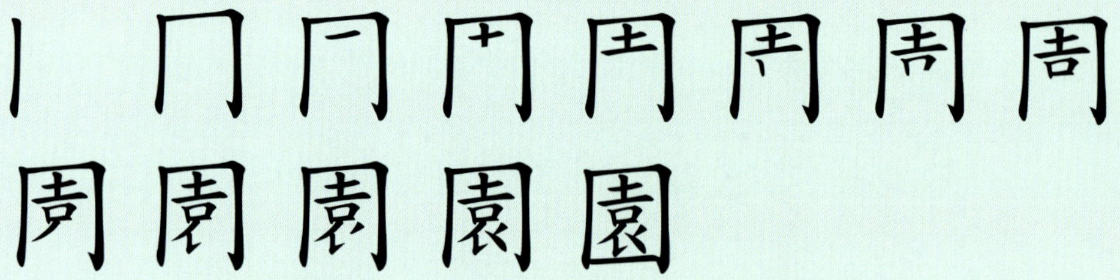

毛 máo fur

第三十五課　請你來我家玩

第三十五課　請你來我家玩

課 文 Text

A: 小文，明天是星期六，你有空嗎？

B: 有啊！你有什麼事(shì)？

A: 明天是我的生日，請你下午三點半來我家，好嗎？

B: 好啊！你還請了誰？

A: 我還請了白瑪麗和白大衛。

B: 太好了！我們要做什麼呢？

A: 我們先(xiān)游泳，再玩電腦遊戲。晚飯吃比薩餅(bǐsàbǐng)和蛋(dàn)糕(gāo)，然後我們可以跳舞(tiàowǔ)，怎麼樣？

B: 太好了！請再告訴(gàosu)我一遍(biàn)你家的地址(dìzhǐ)。

A: 我住在大學路32號。

B: 好！明天見！

A: 明天見！

語 法 Grammar

有空

有空 to have time, to be available, to be free.

你有空嗎？	Are you free?
王老師有空嗎？	Is Teacher WANG available?
爺爺有空嗎？	Is Grandpa free?

什麼事？

什麼事？means "what is the matter?"

你有什麼事？	What's up?
李老師有什麼事？	What's happening with Teacher LI?
白大衛有什麼事？	What does BAI Dawei want?

請…來…

The sentence 請你來我家 is composed of two phrases: 請你 and 來我家, or V1 + object and V2 + object. The first object is the subject of the sentence and the first verb is often causative.

請你來我家。	Please come over to my house.
請老師來我家吃午飯。	Invite the teacher to my house for lunch.
請同學來我家看電視。	Invite my classmates to come over and watch TV.

先…再…

先…再…means "first" A, "then" B, indicating there is a proper or preferred order to the actions or activities mentioned.

我們先游泳再玩電腦。	We will swim first, then play on the computer.
我們先洗手再吃飯。	We wash our hands before we eat.
我們先打乒乓球再打網球。	We play table tennis first and then tennis.

句型練習 Exercises

王老師今天沒有空。

我、下午三點到七點 ⇨ ________________________。

李大中、明天上午 ⇨ ________________________。

白大衛、現在 ⇨ ________________________。

我沒有什麼事。

媽媽 ⇨ ________________________。

白瑪麗 ⇨ ________________________。

他們 ⇨ ________________________。

請你下午三點半來我家玩。

今天中午、教室、找我

⇨ ________________________。

明天上午八點、學校、打籃球

⇨ ________________________。

明年、中國、玩

⇨ ________________________。

快點、飯廳、吃飯

⇨ ________________________。

試試看 Challenge

大衛和小文是好朋友。明天是大衛的生日，他想請小文去他家玩。他給小文打電話，問她明天有沒有空。他想下午先游泳，再玩電腦遊戲，晚上和小文一起吃晚飯。然後，他們一起看電視。小文說可以。大衛很高興。他想明天快點到。

◆生字詞

然後	rán hòu	and then afterwards, subsequently

讀一讀 Reading

我的生日

瑪麗，你好！最近怎麼樣？下星期日是我的生日，好興奮！想請你下午三點到我家參加我的生日會。我也請了大衛，小文和大中。我們會一起玩遊戲，還會游泳，我會點比薩餅給大家吃，快來吧！

小雨

◆生字詞

最近	zuì jìn	recently
興奮	xīng fèn	excited
參加	cān jiā	to participate, take part in
點	diǎn	to order food

Discovering China

文化

Delicious Chinese Food: Moon Cakes 月餅

Eating moon cakes on the 15th day of the 8th month of the lunar calendar is a holiday tradition in China. Moon cakes are a type of pastry that has been eaten in China for a very long time. At first, moon cakes were used as a sacrificial food for the moon goddess. Later, in the Tang Dynasty (618-907), moon cakes became a food that was eaten to celebrate victories, and became associated with the 15th day of the 8th lunar month. The tradition of eating moon cakes while watching the moon during the mid-Autumn festival(中秋節) gradually came to symbolize family togetherness. Today, there are many different styles and flavors of moon cake available in China. There are four main types: Beijing-style, Suzhou-style, Cantonese-style, and Chao Zhou-style. Each type has its own distinct flavor, so you will have to try them all before you decide which one is your favorite!

妙語如珠 Words & Phrases

shān qīng shuǐ xiù 山清水秀	měi bú shèng shōu 美不勝收
Green hills and clear waters; picture-perfect scenery.	Too many beautiful things for the eye to behold.
◆例句： 瑪麗和大中都喜歡旅行，但瑪麗喜歡熱鬧的城市，而大中喜歡山清水秀的地方。	◆例句： 瑪麗第一次參加中國工藝品展覽，各種各樣美不勝收的工藝品讓她眼睛都看不過來了。

◆生字詞

工藝品	gōng yì pǐn	article of handicraft; handiwork
展覽	zhǎn lǎn	exhibit; display; show

認讀字詞 Vocabulary

有空	yǒu kòng	to have time, be available
事	shì	abstract thing, a problem or an event
什麼事	shén me shì	what's up?
還	hái	still, yet
先	xiān	first
再	zài	then, again
明天見	míng tiān jiàn	see you tomorrow

晚飯	wǎn fàn	dinner
比薩餅	bǐ sà bǐng	pizza
蛋糕	dàn gāo	cake
然後	rán hòu	then
跳舞	tiào wǔ	to dance
告訴	gào su	to tell
一遍	yí biàn	once, one time
地址	dì zhǐ	address

百子衣
Hundred Children Embroidery on a Shirt

學寫字 Writing

Write the following characters.

先 xiān before, first　丿 𠂉 ⺧ 生 𫝀 先

再 zài then, again　一 丆 冂 币 再 再

事 shì thing, issue, event　一 𠂇 𠃍 𠃍 𠃍 𠃍 𠃍 事

太 tài too　一 ナ 大 太

明代(1368—1644)繪畫
A Ming Dynasty print

fànguǎn fàn

第三十六課　到中國飯館吃飯

fànguǎn fàn

第三十六課　到中國飯館吃飯

fànguǎn fàn

第三十六課　到中國飯館吃飯

課文 Text

huānyíngguānglín wèi
A：歡迎光臨！請問幾位？

B：三位。

yǐnliào
A：請問，你們要飲料嗎？

bēi chá
B：我要一杯茶。

bīngshuǐ
C：我要冰水，請多放一點冰塊。

chéngzhī
D：你們有橙汁嗎？我要橙汁。

càidān diǎncài
A：這是菜單，請點菜。

xīlánhuā xián
C：我要西蘭花，不要太鹹。

gōngbào jīdīng yuè là
B：我要宮爆雞丁，越辣越好。

suān tián wèidào gǔlǎoròu
D：我喜歡酸甜的味道，我要古老肉。

mǐfàn
A：請問，你們要米飯嗎？

wǎn
B：我們要三碗米飯，謝謝。

fúwùyuán mǎidān gòng
B：服務員，買單。一共多少錢？

A：一共七十九元。

bǎi
B：給你一百元。

zhǎo nín guānglín
A：找您二十一元。謝謝光臨！再見。

B：再見！

語 法 Grammar

請

請 means “please.”

請點菜。	May I take your order?
請結帳。	Check, please
請坐下。	Please have a seat

找…

找… means “give change.”

找您四十塊(錢)。	Here is your change of 40 Kuai.
找您二十五塊(錢)。	Here is your change of 25 Kuai.
找您三十八塊錢。	Here is your change of 38 Kuai.

歡迎光臨

Polite expression used with visitors.

歡迎光臨！ Please come in! Welcome!	謝謝光臨！ Thanks for coming!

句型練習 Exercises

你們要喝橙汁嗎？

點、宮爆雞丁⇨ ________________________？

吃、米飯⇨ ________________________？

結、帳⇨ ________________________？

喝、冰水⇨ ________________________？

一共七十九塊錢。

二十三、個、人⇨ ________________________。

四、條、魚⇨ ________________________。

幾十、塊、錢⇨ ________________________。

三、隻、大熊貓⇨ ________________________。

我們都吃得很高興。

每個人、玩⇨ ________________________。

爺爺和奶奶、看⇨ ________________________。

朋友們、說⇨ ________________________。

試試看 Challenge

我們一家人都愛吃中國菜。星期天晚上，我們一起到一家中國飯館吃飯。因為那天是爸爸的生日，所以他點了他最喜歡吃的菜。爸爸點了北京烤鴨、古老肉、宮爆雞丁、西蘭花和水餃。他還點了一瓶橙汁和一杯茶。媽媽只喝冰水。每樣菜都很好吃。我們都吃得很高興。我送給爸爸一本書，媽媽送給爸爸一條領帶，我和媽媽都祝爸爸生日快樂。爸爸很高興！

◆生字詞

所以	suǒ yǐ	therefore
瓶	píng	bottle
送	sòng	to give
領帶	lǐng dài	tie, neck tie

讀一讀 Reading

去什麼飯館吃什麼飯？去中國飯館，吃中國飯。喝什麼飲料點什麼菜？綠茶、果汁和冰水，烤鴨、水餃、古老肉。一張圓桌一家人，全家團團又圓圓。

◆生字詞

圓	yuán	round
團團圓圓	tuán tuán yuán yuán	family members all gathered together

Discovering China

文化

Culture at the Dining Table 飯桌文化

From ancient times, Chinese people have always been very hospitable. Many of the most important events in life are announced at dinner gatherings of friends and family. In today's fast-paced life, inviting guests over to eat can provide a relaxing break, and is an important way to create and maintain social ties. In the evenings or on weekends, you often find restaurants full, with many people sitting together happily engaged in conversation. Over the course of a meal, people who have not seen each other for a while can catch up, and distant acquaintances can become close friends. It is also common for important things to be decided at a dinner table. Some people call this phenomenon "dining table culture." There is a famous saying, "it doesn't matter what you eat, it matters who you eat with." This really captures the essence of what dining table culture is all about!

傳統美食—餃子
Traditional Chinese food - dumplings

傳統美食—粽子
Traditional Chinese food - Rice wrapped in bamboo leaves

妙 語 如 珠 Words & Phrases

suān tián kǔ là
酸 甜 苦 辣

sour, sweet, bitter, spicy: joys and sorrows of life.

◆例句：

中學生的生活很有趣，不過也有不如意的時候，可以說"酸甜苦辣"，什麼滋味都有。

北京傳統零食—冰糖葫蘆
Traditional snacks in Beijing - Bingtanghulu (candied haw or other fruits on a stick.)

◆生字詞

如意	rú yì	to be satisfied
滋味	zī wèi	experience; feeling

認讀字詞 Vocabulary

飯館	fàn guǎn	restaurant
歡迎光臨	huān yíng guāng lín	welcome (to a store or restaurant)
位	wèi	[a polite measure word for people]
飲料	yǐn liào	beverage, drink
杯	bēi	cup
茶	chá	tea
一杯茶	yì bēi chá	a cup of tea
冰水	bīng shuǐ	ice water
橙汁	chéng zhī	orange juice
菜	cài	dish
菜單	cài dān	menu
點菜	diǎn cài	to order dishes or food
古老肉	gǔ lǎo ròu	sweet and sour pork
宮爆雞丁	gōng bào jī dīng	Kung Pao chicken (spicy fried diced chicken)
西蘭花	xī lán huā	broccoli
鹹	xián	salted; salty
辣	là	spicy
酸	suān	sour
越…越…	yuè...yuè...	the more…the more…
甜	tián	sweet; honeyed
味道	wèi dao	taste; flavor
米飯	mǐ fàn	rice
服務員	fú wù yuán	server
買單	mǎi dān	check for the meal
一共	yí gòng	total
謝謝光臨	xiè xie guāng lín	thank you for coming
找	zhǎo	to give change
您	nín	you [polite form]
百	bǎi	hundred

學寫字 Writing

Write the following characters.

菜 cài dish

一 十 艹 艹 艹 艹 艹 艹
苙 苹 莱 菜

肉 ròu meat

丨 冂 内 内 肉 肉

飯 fàn rice, food

丿 𠂆 𠆢 今 今 今 食 食
飠 飣 飯 飯

中國傳統點心
Traditional Chinese cakes

索引 INDEX

	床	chuáng	bed	28
	春天	chūn tiān	spring	25
	從	cóng	from	31
	粗	cū	thick	34
D	打電話	dǎ diàn huà	to make a phone call	30
	打架	dǎ jià	fight	34
	打一物	dǎ yí wù	take a guess (only used for riddles)	27
	大熊貓	dà xióng māo	giant panda	34
	待著	dāi zhe	stay	34
	袋鼠	dài shǔ	kangaroo	34
	袋子	dài zi	bag, pouch	34
	戴	dài	wear	34
	蛋糕	dàn gāo	cake	35
	等一下	děng yí xià	wait a minute	30
	地址	dì zhǐ	address	35
	點	diǎn	point; o'clock	27/35
	點菜	diǎn cài	to order dishes or food	36
	電話	diàn huà	telephone	30
	電腦	diàn nǎo	computer	25
	電腦遊戲	diàn nǎo yóu xì	computer games	29
	電視	diàn shì	television	29
	肚子	dù zi	stomach	34
	隊	duì	team	28
	對不起	duì bù qǐ	sorry	30
	對方	duì fāng	counterpart; opposite side, other side	32
F	飯館	fàn guǎn	restaurant	36
	飯廳	fàn tīng	dining room	33
	房間	fáng jiān	room	28
	房子	fáng zi	house	33
	放學	fàng xué	school dismissal	27
	分	fēn	minute	27
	分數	fēn shù	score	28
	服務員	fú wù yuán	server	36
G	附近	fù jìn	nearby	34
	高興	gāo xìng	happy	30
	告訴	gào su	to tell	30/35
	根	gēn	[a measure word for long, slim objects]	32

	工藝品	gōng yì pǐn	article of handicraft; handiwork	35
	工作	gōng zuò	work, job	26
	功課	gōng kè	homework	27
	宮爆雞丁	gōng bào jī dīng	Kung Pao chicken (spicy fried diced chicken)	36
	古老肉	gǔ lǎo ròu	sweet and sour pork	36
	故宮	gù gōng	the Forbidden City	30
	故事	gù shi	story	32
	關燈	guān dēng	to turn off the light	33
	光臨	guāng lín	be present	36
H	嗨	hāi	hi	30
	海報	hǎi bào	poster	28
	好感	hǎo gǎn	a good feeling, warm feelings	33
	號碼	hào mǎ	number to indicate the order of something in a series	30
	很多	hěn duō	very many	28
	後面	hòu miàn	behind	25
	花	huā	flower	25/33
	畫畫	huà huà	to draw	31
	歡喜	huān xǐ	happy	31
	歡迎光臨	huān yíng guāng lín	welcome (to a store or restaurant)	36
	還	hái	still, yet	25/35
	還是	hái shì	or	26
	灰姑娘	huī gū niang	Cinderella's Chinese name	26
	回	huí	back, return	27
	回答	huí dá	answer	34
J	家庭主婦	jiā tíng zhǔ fù	homemaker	26
	將來	jiāng lái	in the future	26
	腳	jiǎo	foot	32
	金魚	jīn yú	goldfish	29
	警察	jǐng chá	policeman	26
	拒絕	jù jué	to refuse	34
K	開心	kāi xīn	to be happy	33
	看	kàn	to watch, look at	29
	看電視	kàn diàn shì	to watch television	29
	看見	kàn jiàn	to see	25/34
	看書	kàn shū	to read a book	28
	科學	kē xué	science	31

	棵	kē	[a measure word for plants]	34
	可是	kě shì	but	34
	客廳	kè tīng	living room	33
	課	kè	class	31
	課程	kè chéng	curriculum, course	31
	課程表	kè chéng biǎo	class schedule	31
	啃骨頭	kěn gǔ tou	to gnaw on a bone	29
	空氣	kōng qì	air	25
	孔雀	kǒng què	peacock	34
	酷	kù	awesome, cool	26
L	辣	là	spicy	36
	來來往往	lái lái wǎng wǎng	coming and going	34
	老虎	lǎo hǔ	tiger	34
	老鼠	lǎo shǔ	mouse, rat	25
	理想	lǐ xiǎng	ideal, desirable, desired	28
	裡面	lǐ miàn	inside	25
	歷史	lì shǐ	history	31
	練	liàn	to practice, train	31
	領帶	lǐng dài	tie, neck tie	36
	留言	liú yán	message; to leave a message	33
M	螞蟻	mǎ yǐ	ant	34
	買單	mǎi dān	check for the meal	36
	慢慢	màn màn	slowly	32
	盲	máng	blind	32
	毛	máo	fur	32/34
	帽	mào	cap, hat	28
	沒關係	méi guān xi	it doesn't matter	30
	沒空	méi kòng	not available, no time	30
	每	měi	every	27
	每天	měi tiān	every day	31
	美麗	měi lì	beautiful	33
	美術	měi shù	art	31
	謎語	mí yǔ	riddle	27
	米飯	mǐ fàn	rice	36
	明天見	míng tiān jiàn	see you tomorrow	35
	明星	míng xīng	celebrities, stars	28
	摸	mō	to feel, stroke, touch	32

N	哪裡	nǎ lǐ	where; wherever, all over	25
	那麼	nà me	then	30
	奶奶	nǎi nai	grandmother (paternal)	26
	您	nín	you [polite form]	30/36
P	拍	pāi	to clap	32
	胖胖的	pàng pàng de	chubby, fat	34
	皮球	pí qiú	leather ball, rubber ball	32
	片面	piàn miàn	one-sided, biased	32
	漂亮	piào liàng	beautiful, pretty	34
	瓶	píng	bottle	36
Q	起床	qǐ chuáng	to get out of bed	27
	起居室	qǐ jū shì	family room	33
	前面	qián miàn	in front of	25
	牆	qiáng	wall	28
	青	qīng	green or blue	29
	球場	qiú chǎng	ball court	28
R	然後	rán hòu	and then afterwards, subsequently	35
	熱鬧	rè nao	bustling with activity, lively	34
	如意	rú yì	to be satisfied	36
S	散步	sàn bù	take a walk	29
	沙發	shā fā	sofa	28
	山	shān	mountain	29
	扇子	shàn zi	fan	32
	商人	shāng rén	businessperson	26
	上	shàng	to take; to get on	31
	上班	shàng bān	to go to work	33
	上海	shàng hǎi	Shanghai	28
	上面	shàng miàn	on top of, above	25
	上網	shàng wǎng	go online	28
	少年	shào nián	young adults, teenagers	34
	社會學	shè huì xué	social studies	31
	深夜	shēn yè	late at night	34
	生物	shēng wù	biology	31
	繩子	shéng zi	rope	32
	獅子	shī zi	lion	34
	什麼事	shén me shì	what's up?	35
	事	shì	abstract thing, a problem or an event	35

	手	shǒu	hand	32
	手機	shǒu jī	cell phone, mobile phone	28
	首	shǒu	[a measure word for songs]	31
	書房	shū fáng	study	33
	書架	shū jià	bookshelf	28
	屬	shǔ	belong to (zodiac sign)	28
	數學	shù xué	mathematics	31
	豎	shù	upright	32
	樹	shù	tree, plant	33
	雙	shuāng	two, double, a pair	32
	雙方	shuāng fāng	both sides, two parties	32
	睡覺	shuì jiào	to sleep	27
	送	sòng	to give	36
	酸	suān	sour	36
	所以	suǒ yǐ	therefore	36
T	牠	tā	it [for animals]	29
	它們	tā men	plural form of it	25
	塔	tǎ	pagoda	29
	太好了！	tài hǎo le	that's great!	30
	太極拳	tài jí quán	Tai Chi, shadow boxing	26
	太陽	tài yáng	the sun	27
	討厭	tǎo yàn	be a pain in the neck, to incur dislike; to dislike	33
	體育	tǐ yù	physical education	31
	甜	tián	sweet, honeyed	36
	跳舞	tiào wǔ	to dance	26/35
	聽	tīng	to listen	32
	聽音樂	tīng yīn yuè	listen to music	32
	停	tíng	to stop	27
	團團圓圓	tuán tuán yuán yuán	family members all gathered together	36
	腿	tuǐ	leg	32
W	外面	wài miàn	outside	25
	完	wán	to finish	27
	玩	wán	to play	28
	玩電腦	wán diàn nǎo	to play on the computer	28
	玩具	wán jù	toys	28
	晚飯	wǎn fàn	dinner	35
	忘	wàng	to forget	33

	位	wèi	[polite measure word for people]	36
	味道	wèi dào	taste; flavor	36
	喂	wèi	hello? (on the phone)	30
	衛生間	wèi shēng jiān	bathroom	33
	聞	wén	to smell	32
	臥室	wò shì	bedroom	33
	午餐	wǔ cān	lunch	31
	舞廳	wǔ tīng	dance hall	34
	物理	wù lǐ	physics	31
X	西瓜	xī guā	watermelon	25
	西蘭花	xī lán huā	broccoli	36
	洗衣房	xǐ yī fáng	laundry room	33
	下	xià	next	30
	下面	xià miàn	under, below	25
	嚇得	xià de	afraid	34
	先	xiān	first	32/35
	鹹	xián	salted, salty	36
	現在	xiàn zài	now	27
	香味	xiāng wèi	sweet smell	32
	像	xiàng	look like, resemble	34
	小學生	xiǎo xué shēng	elementary school student	26
	寫作	xiě zuò	writing	31
	謝謝光臨	xiè xie guāng lín	thank you for coming	36
	新	xīn	new	30
	新鮮	xīn xiān	fresh	25
	興奮	xīng fèn	excited	35
	熊	xióng	bear	33
	選	xuǎn	to select, choose	31
	學期	xué qī	term, semester, school term	25
Y	牙齒	yá chǐ	tooth, teeth	32
	眼鏡	yǎn jìng	eyeglasses	34
	演員	yǎn yuán	actor	26
	養	yǎng	to raise; to provide for	33
	姚明	yáo míng	a famous basketball player	28
	咬	yǎo	to bite	32
	爺爺	yé ye	grandfather (paternal)	26
	一杯茶	yì bēi chá	a cup of tea	36

	一遍	yí biàn	once, one time	35
	一共	yí gòng	total	36
	一家人	yì jiā rén	a family	29
	一起	yì qǐ	together	26/29
	一樣	yí yàng	the same, alike	31
	一直	yì zhí	always	34
	衣櫃	yī guì	closet (for clothing)	28
	醫生	yī shēng	doctor	26
	因為	yīn wèi	because	30/34
	音樂	yīn yuè	music	31
	飲料	yǐn liào	beverage, drinks	36
	用	yòng	to use	32
	游來游去	yóu lái yóu qù	to swim back and forth	29
	遊戲	yóu xì	game	28/29
	有空	yǒu kòng	to have time, be available	35
	有趣	yǒu qù	interesting	34
	又	yòu	as well, also	34
	羽毛	yǔ máo	feather	34
	寓言	yù yán	fable	32
	原因	yuán yīn	reason	26
	圓	yuán	round	36
	越…越…	yuè...yuè...	the more...the more...	36
	閱讀	yuè dú	reading; to read	31
	運動員	yùn dòng yuán	athlete	26
Z	雜誌	zá zhì	magazine	28
	再	zài	then, again	35
	在家	zài jiā	at home	30
	早飯	zǎo fàn	breakfast	27
	早上	zǎo shang	morning	27
	責任	zé rèn	duty, responsibility, obligation	32
	展覽	zhǎn lǎn	exhibit; display; show	35
	展示	zhǎn shì	reveal; show	34
	站住，舉起手來！	zhàn zhù, jǔ qǐ shǒu lái	Stop! Hands up!	26
	張	zhāng	piece [a measure word for paper]	28
	找	zhǎo	to give change	36
	真	zhēn	really	29
	爭吵	zhēng chǎo	to quarrel	32
	正中	zhèng zhōng	right in the middle	27

知道	zhī dào	to know	32
蜘蛛	zhī zhū	spider	34
職業	zhí yè	profession, professional	26
中鋒	zhōng fēng	center (position in basketball)	28
中間	zhōng jiān	middle	33
中學	zhōng xué	secondary school	26
中學生	zhōng xué shēng	secondary school student	26
主	zhǔ	master, main	33
柱	zhù	post, upright, pillar	32
祝福	zhù fú	blessing, well wishing	31
滋味	zī wèi	experience; feeling	36
紫	zǐ	purple	31
自然	zì rán	naturally; of course; nature	26
最近	zuì jìn	recently	35
做	zuò	to do, work	26
做功課	zuò gōng kè	to do homework	27